D0970427

Ivan
THE TERRIBLE
& Ivan THE FOOL

Also by Yevgeny Yevtushenko

THE FACE BEHIND THE FACE
LOVE POEMS
STOLEN APPLES
BRATSK STATION AND OTHER NEW POEMS
POEMS
SELECTED POEMS

PRECOCIOUS AUTOBIOGRAPHY

Ivan
THE TERRIBLE
& Ivan THE FOOL
YEVGENY·YEVTUSHENKO

TRANSLATED BY DANIEL WEISSBORT

RICHARD MAREK PUBLISHERS
NEW YORK

Library of Congress Cataloging in Publication Data

Evtushenko, Evgenii Aleksandrovich.
  Ivan the Terrible and Ivan the Fool.

  Translation of Ivanovskie sitšsy.
  I. Title.
PG3476.E96I913   891.7'1'44   79-21282
ISBN 0-399-90064-0
PRINTED IN THE UNITED STATES OF AMERICA

TRANSLATOR'S INTRODUCTION

In his long poem, *Calico from Ivanovo*, translated here as *Ivan the Terrible and Ivan the Fool*, Yevtushenko has, it seems to me, produced a kind of Soviet epic. This epic endeavour is traceable from the outset of his career and his "optimistic" perception of the original—and recoverable—humanistic revolutionary impulse finds here a distinctive historical and symbolic embodiment.

Of course, the "epic" glorification of Soviet achievements, the retelling in heroic terms of Soviet history is, to say the least, not uncommon in Soviet literature. But, after the early revolutionary enthusiasm had run its course, the prescriptive pressure behind such works produced little more than bombast and rhetoric. It was, indeed, against such hollow verbiage, such petty-bourgeois versification, programmatic and ritualistic, that the new poets of the post-Stalin period like Yevgeny Vinokurov and Boris Slutsky—together with survivors from the war and pre-war periods like Olga Berggolts and Anna Akhmatova—set themselves. The anti-heroic, "minimal" poetry of postwar Eastern and Central Europe, with its bare, essential language, stripped of Romantic–Symbolist accretions in response to the stark and deadly experiences of the period, was echoed even in Russia by the verse of such as Vinokurov and Slutsky, who were trying to recover that truth to experience that had been so criticized in Akhmatova, condemned in the postwar cultural freeze.

However, this poetry represented only one trend. Shortly after came Voznesensky and Yevtushenko who, in world as well as national terms, swiftly acquired the status of celebrities. This was partly, no doubt, due to a somewhat misleading identification of them with the "angry young men" of generation-conscious Western Europe. Nevertheless, this characterization did contain a grain of truth. The Khrushchevite Fifties, with a leader who eventually inherited the old dictator's monolithic power but not his monolithic predictability, embodied a conscious effort at differentiation from what had preceded. Khrushchev, necessarily appealing in his own rise to power to a wider constituency—though he also represented the old guard, the *apparatchiki* survivors of the Purges, and was not, one would think, ideally fitted to preside over the dissolution of a system he had so successfully exploited—nevertheless was instrumental in bringing about conditions that allowed a gulf to open between the generations, much as it had done in postwar Western Europe. In so far as Yevtushenko and other young poets were hopeful of change, they might loosely be equated with those youthful class rebels in England described by John Osborne in his famous play.

However, the anti-dogmatists, the reformers, in this instance were far from being entirely forward-looking. In the wake of the revelations of Stalinist atrocities, of official, if partial, acknowledgement of crimes committed by the state, or in the name of the state, with the search for catharsis or absolution threatening to sweep away the whole edifice, to lead to a total rejection of the Soviet experience, an effort to reassert positive revolutionary values became discernible. Criticism of the bad old ways continued, but it was carried out in terms of an adherence to so-called Leninist norms. In the symbology of the times, Stalin was revealed as the Antichrist, one might say, to Lenin's Christ. This attempt to make sense out of Soviet history, of the agony of revolution, civil war, and political purges, was reflected among some of the young poets, notably Yevtushenko, in a kind of revolutionary romanticism, harking back to the original ideals of revolution that had patently been betrayed but were not necessarily invalidated. It was this idealistic nostalgia, with the challenge they were at the same time putting to the compromised old guard (including Khrushchev), that accounted for the great popularity of poets like Yevtushenko. Though he also wrote very touching lyrics on more intimate themes, Yevtushenko, together with his contemporary Voznesensky, found himself the tribune of a large section of Soviet youth. His words, as the cliché goes, awoke echoes in the people, at least the young people, and those echoes further encouraged the poet in his efforts.

10

The link between mass audience and solitary poet is one that only the Beatniks in the West have experienced and enjoyed. It is a link based not on intimate self-revelation, or even communal recognition of a private world, so much as on the sharing of a common historical and cultural experience. In this relationship, the poet truly does become a kind of unofficial tribune, giving voice to popular aspirations, telling the people their own story, drawing on the past but also projecting into the future in a kind of collective imaginative effort. This model of poet as tribune is one very alien to us now—so alien, indeed, that we may often fail to recognize such poets as poets at all. After a period in the Fifties and Sixties when the Beats fed the Whitmanesque aspirations and hopes of the young, reaching out to mass audiences, poetry in the West seems to have returned to its traditional, one might almost say post-Romantic, stance of self-questioning and self-doubt. In this climate and in a period when politically there seems little cause for optimism—the real disillusionment set in with the collapse of the student movements in 1968, the abrupt termination of the Czechoslovak experiment in "socialism with a human face", the revelation of corruption in high places with Watergate, etc.—it is hard for us to look upon the vast sweep Yevtushenko envisages in the present poem with a less than jaundiced eye. We are in a period when the epic cannot be said to be flourishing; or, if the beginnings of a new epic impulse are to be recognized, it is surely in the verse of such as Vasko Popa of Yugoslavia, who has, with the help of a kind of folk surrealism, dismembered the world as we know it and is now magically and, indeed, majestically reassembling it.

All this might lead the Western reader to regard poems like the present one as little better than propaganda—propaganda, perhaps, with some fine passages and skilfully versified (few would deny Yevtushenko's great technical virtuosity), but propaganda none the less. Yet one of Yevtushenko's pervasive characteristics has been his ability openly to confront, in an almost journalistic way, major historical and social issues. In so doing, he brings himself into the picture, but the self he brings in is that of a modern man, perhaps less questioning than his Western counterpart, but recognizably human all the same. And, paradoxically, this

11

self, whose own spiritual history unfolds in shadowy counterpoint to the material, is precisely that of the epic story-teller. The human voice behind the poem becomes the *vox populi* which Yevtushenko also "impersonates" so successfully in his celebrated stage performances. With increasing skill, the poet has undertaken this task of epic story-telling, but without losing his openness—without, in other words, succumbing to the temptation or danger of identifying totally with his material, merging with it and so becoming a mere cog in the propaganda machine. Yevtushenko has somehow, it seems to me, turned the tables on a system where propaganda has been accorded the status of epic.

To make the present poem intelligible to the English reader without a background in Russian history and the Russian folk tradition, I have chosen to provide detailed notes rather than an elaborate historical introduction, because that method seemed to me more appropriate to the nature of the poem itself. *Ivan the Terrible and Ivan the Fool* is a complex dramatic reconstruction of Russian history, centring on the creation in 1905 of the Ivanovo-Voznesensk soviet, but moving in a fashion more impressionistic than chronological among various periods: those of Ivan the Terrible, Peter the Great, Nicholas II and the abdication, and the 1905 Revolution—all this set against a background of the Russian folk epos, with its traditional character of Ivan the Fool. The poem is a comment on major aspects of Russian history, and the notes are intended to present that history and to explain specific references in a more direct and objective fashion, to provide the reader with the information that most Russian readers of the poem would have.

The decision to change the title of the poem for its publication in English should, perhaps, be explained here. The original title, *Calico from Ivanovo*, relates the poem in a characteristically Yevtushenkian fashion to a specific incident. Ivanovo-Voznesensk, a large textile centre, was also from the 1880s (see note on l. 381) an important centre of the labour movement. The 1905 strike and the establishment, though abortive, of one of the first Soviets of Workers' Deputies becomes, in Yevtushenko's poem, emblematic of the general revolutionary impulse for change. Historical personages such as Mikhail Frunze (l. 497) figure in the poem as examples of those genuine "heroes" of the people who were betrayed by Stalin and the Party *apparatchiki* of the post-Leninist period. The change of title has meant sacrificing the historical specificity of the original, but since the reference to Ivanovo could make no immediate impact in translation, I felt justified in substituting a title that would be more resonant in the English context and which emphasizes rather the epic nature of the work.

In the poem, the name "Ivan" is used in a number of ways—and I hope these have been sufficiently elucidated in the notes. However, two *principal* poles are set up, those of Ivan the Terrible (the historic, if epicized, Tsar Ivan IV) and Ivan the Fool, one of the principal characters in the Russian folk epos. For Yevtushenko, the Fool is symbolic of the people, or more accurately, the growing popular consciousness. The Fool is no fool, nor is he a holy fool, but an embryonically all-powerful agent, as against the autocrat who is the *actual* holder of power. But if anyone understands the Fool, Ivan—understands and rightly fears him—it is this same autocrat, Ivan. These two Ivans, the intertraffic between them, and the way the transference of power from one to the other is constantly frustrated, is the underlying subject of the poem. The autocrat, Ivan the Terrible, degenerates over the centuries into the weak yet inflexible Nicholas II, while the Fool grows in consciousness to become a Frunze.

It is significant that of the two elemental types of Russian fairy-tale hero, Ivan the Prince and Ivan the Fool, Yevtushenko should have chosen the latter. The Fool is usually depicted as unreliable, undertaking the traditional heroic quest for selfish reasons, while the Prince's quest is altruistic and noble. Both heroes are successful in the outcome, but the Prince's success is deserved, unlike that of the Fool. The heroic immaculacy of the Prince would clearly not have served the poet's purposes. On the other hand, his depiction of the Fool is not the traditional one; he represents, rather, a composite hero with traditional elements. Yevtushenko has, in fact, created an epic hero for Soviet Russia.

Lastly, a few words about the translation itself. All translations involve compromises and losses, and it is the translator's responsibility to try to identify some of these. Generally speaking, I adhere to a middle path in translation: that is, I work with the literal or literalistic raw material, derived directly from the source, rather than with my own interpretation or elaboration of it. Of course, the discussion as to what exactly "literal" translation is could be drawn out endlessly—in an important sense, a literal version is quite impossible—but the point here is that an attempt is made to set up a current between source and target, composed of elements as specific as possible. The translation, while "it can be read on its own", is not a generic entity but remains always linked to its source—and not merely in the way that the whole of literature, in spite of linguistic boundaries, may be said to form a whole. What is involved here, perhaps, is a kind of minimal theory of translation, where change is tolerated only when absolutely essential. Again, of course, it is all a question of negotiation between how much change is felt to be necessary, on the one hand, and what the target language permits, on the other; and there is also the more mundane or realistic question of the nature of the audience.

In this latter connection, it would be possible, just possible, to write a poem *after* Yevtushenko, transposing all the material into the English context, with an English folk sub-hero, with episodes from King John, Richard III, Charles I and Cromwell, the Chartists, the postwar Atlee government, intimations of a new post-imperial Britain in the Festival of Britain, etc. This would clearly involve writing a distinct and different poem. It would be to naturalize the poem, making certain gestures in its direction, but concentrating on its *immediate* accessibility to an English audience, though even with so free a translation the question of greater or lesser literalness arises. It is this kind of approach that the great Augustan translators of the classics, Pope and Johnson, exploited to the full.

While there is an excellent argument for this type of translation—or "imitation", as it has been called—from a remote time which can be only problematically reconstructed even with the most painstaking scholarship, it would seem

14

less justifiable in the context of the same age and closely related cultures. In addition, we have become less ethnocentric and more curious about the "otherness" of other cultures. Rather than naturalize, or "English", as the Elizabethans have it, transporting the original to the reader, translation may take the opposite course. It may try to expand the target language to accommodate the new foreignness, it may try to bring the reader to the source, not just its "spirit" but its very body.

At the opposite end of the spectrum is the literal approach, that "blind superstition", in Dryden's words, of the automatic transferability of words between languages. In its medieval context, absolutely literal translation produced often quite unintelligible texts in the target language and it was challenged very early in the history of translation. A less extreme version of literal translation might be described as *literate*. Here, the target language employed is the standard language of the day. The translated text is readable, comprehensible, but aspires only to conveying content, not (among other things) form. Both fashion and the exigencies of publishing deadlines have contributed to the proliferation of this kind of translation.

Of course, the above is a somewhat schematic account of the options available to the translator, probably raising more questions than it answers, and what can be claimed for one translation method can probably also be claimed for others. It does, however, perhaps help to establish some sort of context for the decisions made in the present translation. Since one aim is maximally to convey the specific content, I have, as has been said, resorted to an extensive use of notes. Ideally I would like the reader to read through the poem once or twice with the notes, and then again without them, with the information or enough of it assimilated. But another aim, if of marginally lower priority, is to approximate to the form, diction, tone as exactly as possible, that is without compromising the sense or meaning of the original. In the present case, form and tone were a large part of the poem, which is, as I have noted, a kind of epic, but also a collage of various classical and traditional, popular and courtly prosodic conventions.

15

To say that mastery of these forms, a flexible control—though with occasional longueurs—of the language, an often brilliantly inventive use of rhyme, characterize the original is also to define the weaknesses of the translation. However, lacking, among other things, the phonic resources of an inflected language, what I have tried to do is at least to *reflect* the original; the translation, to borrow a metaphor, may be seen as the underside of a rich tapestry. Where it has been possible to compensate without abandoning my general literal direction, I have done so, but I have resisted the temptation to cut my language free and adopt more familiar English modes. What remains is maybe awkward enough to provoke the occasional grimace. As against that it does not represent a smoothing out. This, in my view, would have been the worse traducement.

Lastly, it is a pleasure to record the large debt I owe to Max Hayward, who took time off from his own busy schedule to read the original draft and make numerous invaluable suggestions. In addition he also indicated where he felt notes were necessary and outlined the contents of many of these notes. The responsibility for the final version remains, of course, mine alone.

London, July 1978   DANIEL WEISSBORT

16

Ivan
THE TERRIBLE
& Ivan THE FOOL

1

From the time when he was laid
                              in the cradle
                                             Fool Ivan
had two eyes of cornflower blue,
                              sly and lively,
                                             full of fun.
In the freckled wheaten fields
                              of his face these flowers grew,
as across the vast expanse
                              of our Russian land befooled.
And these flowers, gazing hard,
                              shook each lordly manor
                                             home.   5
And these flowers whispered: "Ye
                              shall yet reap what ye
                              have sown . . ."
And bell-like were the fists
                              of Ivan, Ivan the Fool,
as they filled out,
                   frisked and frolicked,
                                      though they were
                                      a vassal's tools.
And the tavern called them to it
                              in the shindies and the
                                             battles,
so, like savage dogs, the peasants there
                                      might fight and
                                      swing the bottle,   10
but even that hag vodka
                   coated them herself
with the pre-industrial copper
                              of a mind grown to full size.

21

His ears were pricked. Ivan, in short,

                        was always on his
                                 guard.

When, like a rag within the mouth,

                   the tongue's a stump of
                               lard,

and a pike lifts up the tongue itself

                    above the axe's arc,   15

you may extirpate the cry, it's true,

                        but the mindful ears
                               still hark.

You may maim a person's mouth—

                     you'll have trouble with
                               the ears.

If you cannot speak, you still

                  are at liberty to hear.

And Ivan, Ivan the Fool's

               orphaned back

                       turned blue, and
                               yet

it grew wiser too,

           and wiser,

                  from the beatings that it got.   20

You may whack the brains and senses

                    out of any oafish
                         blockhead,

but you cannot beat the marrow

                    from the spine where it is
                           lodged.

The people's brain is born

                 not beneath the brow or
                       forelock,

but within the tired backbone,

                 in the whip-tormented
                     back . . .

Once a seven-headed serpent

                 infiltrated Ivan's dream,   25

and the cursed one whispered: "Mind you're

                                not too clever!
                        Do
                not seem
to be. All the Tsars and boyars

                fear the brain more than
                                sedition,
which is why they grind it down

                in their towers and their
                                dungeons!
Surrender up your senses, gratis,

                to debauchery.
For the punishment of brains,

                the block's absorbed no end
                                of trees!   30
I'm not about to loose

                your brain, with neck askew,
from the noose. Not brains but cunning's

                                what our Russian
                                people value.
Go unclothed and without shoes,

                live in silence, sideways
                                on,
among other fools a fool,

                better show some sense, Ivan . . ."
But Ivan grinned at the serpent:

                "Don't speak for Russia,
                                snake,   35
I don't know how to be one,

                but a fool I'll imitate.
Brains should not be advertised.

                So I do not get confused,
I'll invent a likely story,

                with a hero called the Fool.
Don't compare me to a fool though,

                capering with a
                                tambourine.

                                23

This tale will be as sticky
                    as the swamps of Susanin.   40
Yes, so many clever people
                    come to grief over this tale
of Russia's poor and wretched
                    and Ivan, Ivan the Fool!
A secret wit is wiser
                    than a show-off, show-all mind,
just as sometimes kvass is stronger,
                              makes your nose
                              twitch more
                              than wine.
And my mind addressed me: "Friend", it said,
                              "keep your
                              thinking
                              quiet   45
for the mighty celebrations,
                    like a knife for cutting pies."
Like an axe wrapped in a cloth,
                    but sharpened and made
                              ready,
a mind put by stays keen—
                    so I'll take it nice and steady.
Let it lie there just like me,
                    clothed in tatters and in rags,
until all the Ivans
                    take up their axes . . .   50
I am gaunter than Koshchey,
                    I am poorer than
                              Koshchey,
more immortal than Koshchey,
                    perhaps because of sour
                              shchi.
Nothing's going to get me down—
                    I come of peasant stock.
And like shchi made out of axes,
                    I'll cook up a rebel pot!

      24

I'll leap into the shchi
                        with all my lice upon me,   55
but I'll issue from it whole—
                        it's my own and it won't scald
                                                me.
It is hard to keep pretending
                        that I'm just a country
                                        bumpkin,
and it's risky acting silly,
                        since one might *become* a ninny.
But we'll make you all repent
                        bitterly throughout the ages
all the cheating that you did,
                        making fools of us, not
                                        sages . . ."   6o

2

Lord Ivan Vasilevich the Terrible
seldom risked a dewy constitutional.
More often across carpets, marble floors,
over corpses he squelched and tramped through gore.
Lord Ivan Vasilevich the Terrible   65
seldom listened on a starry eve to nightingales.
No nightingale's, the Tsar's nocturnal birdsong
was the screams of folk in towers and in dungeons.
But one night the dreaded sovereign was aroused
not by his upset stomach—
                                    this was soused   70
in mead and bloated from fish patties—
but by a nightingale's anonymous ditty.
Thin was that voice but animate,
as after an execution, on the chipped axe blade,
a stray hair stirs—
                                    and the Tsar heard its lament   75
in the deep shadows:
                    "Repent,
                                repent . . ."

29

And in his nightshirt the monarch left the chamber,
barefoot into the garden went, and listened
fearfully to the song's accusation
issuing thence as if by miracle.   80
And the Tsar thought, tearing away convolvulus:
"Aye, it is true that nightingales have other passions.
I'm not endowed with what the nightingale has.
What's mine is power, exercised by right, God-given.
And if it's not from God, this power, but rather   85
the devil?"
                    He shuddered:
                                        "Heresy . . .
You're an apostate, nightingale,
                                        a wretched liar.
Power is divine.
                    I'll not lose faith in that!"
The Tsar, entangled in the garden, as in a thicket,
hunted the singer with claws drawn,   90
breathed hard and said to the nightingale:
                                                  "I'm sick at
heart, believing in no one at all . . ."
And, colliding on the narrow path with his Tsar,
Viskovaty,
                    clerk to the council of boyars,
pretended that he hadn't heard a thing   95
(though, in the end, it's true, this did not save him).
And the oprichniks, stinking of raw vodka,
shook the apple trees and birches in the hue
and cry, hacking away with pole-axes to no purpose
at amethystine pearls of dew.   100
Viskovaty made a cunning attempt
to end this avicular torment.
If, houndlike,
                    you can sense a monarch's wrath,
then even a nightingale may be put on the spot.
"My Lord",
                    said the clerk Viskovaty,   105

30

with his furtive air,
                    and falsely hearty,
"I have my doubts about the printing trade:
We must be careful not to overlook mistakes."

Now, Lord Ivan Vasilevich the Terrible
was, after all, godfather to Ivan Fyodorov.   110
He'd personally lay the paper on the press
and, hiding a childlike smile, examine it
and show it to his guests from overseas,
saying: "See what Ivans our Russia breeds . . ."

So, the Tsar scowled now:
                    "What did you have in mind?"   115
"Well,
        it is really the whole enterprise.
If books are to increase faster and faster,
then the serfs will grow to be just like their master.
And what if Ivashka suddenly decides
to print subversive writings on the side?   120
There's a danger
                in every handwrit word,
but printed,
            it sings louder than that bird—
it would not give you any peace at all . . ."
The Tsar thought hard:
                    "I'll hear no idle talk . . .
Clerk, are there subversive texts or not?"   125
"There may be . . .
                Tsar, close down the shop!"
"And our Ivan?
                My hand's too tired to beat him."
"We can drop a hint
                and on his journey speed him!"

Lord Ivan Vasilevich the Terrible
was clever,
            though he wasn't reckoned so.   130

31

That night he drank and drank,
                              his face was sullen,
but the red wine from France brought him no comfort.
If you govern ignorant folk
                    you yourself become a
                              blockhead.
But if they're literate,
                    you're better off dead.
Should he cut down the apple tree
                              and cherry,   135
so the bird should no more offend his hearing?
It would repair
                    to broom and willow,
                              if he did.
The Tsar was kind.
                    He said:
                    "Then drop a hint."

And so they did.
                    Fyodorov Ivan
bade farewell to the royal printing house   140
and quickly slipped the type into his bag—
that it was spared showed quite uncommon lenience.
He smoothed out the edges of a stray sheet—
on it was laid the nailed impression
of an oprichnik's metal heel,   145
mark of his sovereign Lord's appreciation.
They had not found subversive documents,
but for the oprichniks the alphabet
itself was subversive,
                              containing salt
rather than the cunning of delusive mead.   150
Cruelly wounded, consumed by grief,
Ivan procured a cart,
                    and left the court,
and maybe for the first time in his life
allowed himself to think his secret thoughts:

32

"How happy I was in my Tsar to trust,   155
bending my head before him dutifully!
I did not irritate the State, nor judge,
but that has not stopped it from judging me.
In the State's limpid gaze, I swear—
though I do not expect a just and fair trial—   160
such perfidious treatment's not deserved,
for I myself have never been deceitful.
I tried to love you, State, my one desire
to be of service, but I knew
that I would cease to be if I   165
cringed like a cowardly dog before you.
State, you are serfs and nobles, domain
of denunciation, fawning, enmity.
The serf can't simultaneously entertain
feeling for State and country . . ."   170

Great Gutenberg,
                would you have understood
the joys life offers to your Russian colleague,
who, banned from Moscow, sits atop his cart,
the letters of the alphabet for luggage?
You would have understood, kirsch drinker, in your cups, 175
Ivan, unheard, sobbing into his sleeve,
when he was shooed away, just like a pup—
lucky for him
                he was let off so cheap!
But where was he to drag his type-face, where
now his homeless printing plaques?   180
Ivan grimaced, in dumb despair,
like so many other unknown namesakes.
Who can accept abroad,
                who grasp
that Russians are not simply beasts of burden?
Prince Kurbsky?
                No. He's but a counter-tsar.   185

33

And the Swedes are Swedes,
                    when all is said and done.
Mud, mud everywhere,
                    you wade through mud.
Freedom, under suspicion, is locked in gaol.
And even Russians cannot live in Russia,
though without Russia, life's intolerable.   190
The clouds, like psaltery players, strayed above
the road which, smelling of damp earth,
meandered on and on, with twists and turns,
like the tortuous story of Ivan the Fool.
Suddenly from the thicket rose a whistle   195
and horsemen swept in at a gallop,
leaping on to the road before the printer—
no brooms, however,
                    no dog-masks at their saddle.
One of these riders,
                    evidently their head,
so badly scalded, it looked like the mange,   200
snorting through torn nostrils, said:
"If it's gold you have,
                    deliver up, make haste!"
Hotly slashing the sacking with his sword,
he saw the lead:
                    "What's that?"
                                        "It's letters."
"What for?"
          "For books."
                              "And books, what are they for?"   205
"For you, you fool . . . ,"
                    the printer muttered.
"For me, oho!"
                    The chief laughed out aloud.
"I'd have been at my wit's end
if, with my ragged piece, I'd tried to sniff out
the sense of what your letters meant.   210
But this lead you've got here's fine—

we'll make bullets from it for our arquebuses . . ."
"Never!"
                    "Prepare to die, then."
                              "All right. I'll die—
and you'll never be free of your troubles."
"Who's free? Even the thief's not free.   215
Nor is an unfrocked priest—
                    ask this one here.
So in what manner can I be free? . . ."
"What manner? Why, through books, through letters . . ."
It struck the chief at last,
                    this **was** no merchant.
Gold such as this he'd be ashamed to seize.   220
Lead, not earth
              soiled the printer's hands.
This lead, however,
                    was his soil, it seemed.
"Live . . . ,"
              said the chief, climbing back on his horse.
"Let these—what d'you call them—letters be loosed,
and not from arquebuses, but so   225
there's blood to tell the tale,
                    not cranberry juice! . . ."
"You'll never settle anything with blood . . . ,"
the printer sighed.
                  "Well me, I don't eat grass,"
grinned the chief.
                  "My name is Vanka Shish."
"I'm Ivan too."
                  "So's our accursed Tsar.   230
The news has reached us wandering folk
that there's been sent, from across the ocean,
an Ivangel—or some such book.
Is it about the Tsar or all Ivans?"
"E-vangel's what it's called . . ."
                              "A fraud, I see . . .   235
We are not good enough for books, my guess is.

35

Print us some books, Ivan, and maybe we
will learn one day to use those letters . . ."
They galloped off,
                              lashing their horses' flanks,
and this is what it signified—   240
illiterate as they were, their anger
made the people want to read and write.
"Ivangel too will one day have its turn . . . ,"
Ivan thought. "The people will rise . . . ,"
while behind him
                              the letters in the wagon   245
rumbled,
            centuries ahead of time.

3

"Russischer Ivan.
Grossischer *idiot* . . . ,"
growled
     a mud-stained Lefort,
grovelling at Peter's boot.   250
And the Tsar looked askance at him,
                    as if
to crush him with his look,
                like a coin in his fist,
while inspecting
          wenches
             and fortifications:
"I too am Ivan,
          though I'm known to the nation
as Peter."
        With such a Tsar, better watch your words: 255
he'll put you to death—
           dump you straight in the sod!
Behind Peter's the shade of a special Ivan—
the terrible one.
And even Menshikov Aleksashka

has Ivan-the-Terrible mannerisms.
Take care, take care,
                          or he'll roll you flat,
though he grabs
                     without regard for the size,
with hands still so sticky from dough and fat,
that you want to hiss:
                    "Give me a pie!"
Lefort was abashed—he flopped into a sleigh,   265
and his Adam's apple
                          gave a spasmic
                                        jolt,
as if Ivan's staff, like a stake,
had been driven
                     into his throat.
And Lefort couldn't sleep that night
in the sleigh, as it jogged along.   270
On the rack of fear, his spine
cracked, like a bug stepped on.
Snow and filth lay in equal measure
like a quagmire over the land of Rus.
And so Lefort thought:
                    "Can we ever   275
free the country from this foul muck?
All these sweaty efforts and more,
to propel Russia forward at a rush
are possible only through horrible torture
and torture means still more muck.   280
Where am I? In a terrible cabinet
of curiosities, with blood-slimed chains,
where screaming hunks of flesh
hang from hooks in twisted shapes.
The Tsar does not countenance *felos de se*,   285
any more than the common highwayman,
but Anna, in her woman's way,
senses the Tsar's self-immolation.
In torture he has shown some erudition

40

but suddenly on his face there appears   290
a look of doom as with one of his own Streltsy
who has not yet been cut down by him . . ."
Lefort sighed:
                    "Peter, of course,
has talent but he is a tyrant.
For Europe he's still too much the boor.   295
As he admits,
                    he's still Ivan."
Lefort drew a bearskin rug over
the Utrecht velvet of his breeches,
but the fear crept in even so,
surreptitious, but as cold and bleak.   300
Lefort again recalled,
                    recoiling
from the fateful sights of slaughter,
all the uncrowned Ivans as well
who made his blood turn to water.
Already, in the days of Peter,   305
flickering in mutiny,
the ripening power of the serf
into the royal yeast was kneaded.
All the navvies,
                    all the miners,
who'd exchanged their hoes for picks,   310
at times looked so ominous—
not like Ivan the Fool a bit.
Hardly human,
                    more like replicas,
but if a serf even so
could look out from under his brow so darkly,   315
then what might be stirring within?
The thought struck Lefort as he was jarred
by one of those eternal potholes:
"With the pick given them by the Tsar,
they'll dig his grave as well!"   320
And this thought, with its deathly chill,

that had no place in his report,
was followed:
             "In Russia any Ivan is

                             terrible . . ."
That night sleep did not come to Lefort.

4

Oh, terrible Ivans,

                starving and tattered,   325

you were the real Ivans

                    that mattered.

Oh, terrible Ivans,

              parentless

                  and throneless,

didn't rule from the Kremlin,

                    though you built that palace.

You didn't depend on a drunken oprichnina

but the plough, which Tsar's hands never knew.   330

Dearer to you than the iron-tipped sceptre

was the standing corn

                  and the lively grasshopper.

But you've long known how to scowl terribly,

from under Muromets's shaggy brow,

                    at your enemy.

And like Buslayev,

                you took pride in the dread custom,   335

when great Novgorod sounded its tocsin.

Oh, terrible Ivans,

                without sceptre or staff,

you knew innocent revel,

                  ingenuous dance,

but your sinews were stretched to breaking point,

and from them burst

              Razin

                  and Bolotnikov,   340

and Pugachov, calling for rebellion,

                  undressed,

showed the marks of a king on his bare flesh.
Oh, illiterate nation,
                    your lives went unrecorded,
but to the crackle of rushlights,
                              you brought forth Ivan
                                        Fyodorov.
The First Printer,
                    wiping his type-face with a rag,   345
was an Ivan the Terrible,
                         though unconscious of the
                                        fact,
for the Russian word—
                    especially when printed—
can roar like thunder
                    and make palaces quiver.
Yes, the Russian word,
                    chiseled
                         and beaten,
burst through with Pushkin
                         and exploded in leaflets,   350
but perhaps,
          even before the formation of the nation,
the people wrote
                birch-bark proclamations . . .
This is the worst
                danger to authority,
for princes and princelings
                         always fear publicity.
But when publicity's half silenced
                         and in hiding,   355
it fills with an awesome dynamite.
And if a word
          is stuffed with dynamite,
then there's no revolution
                         it cannot ignite!
Terrible Ivans,
          yet more terrible you became,

46

when your ancestral villages
                         you left for the machine.   360
Secretly afraid,
               he who gave you the pick,
                                great Peter
was proletarian Russia's
                         terrible progenitor.
After all the agitation,
                  the strivings,
                           the errors,
Russia gave birth to the proletarian era.
A path led the workers
                     to the Tsar's drinking-house.   365
They were shot at Lena
                    and the Winter Palace.
And they were already reading Lenin and Plekhanov,
and pasting up Bolshevik proclamations.
And they grew,
            like a black-clad Ivan the Terrible
of the smoking Putilov works,
                          dispatched bosses to hell,   370
and from distraught Morozovs
                        accepted offers
of money
        for Ivan's mutinous coffers.
What can they all do,
                   the Zubatovs and the Gapons
with the deep veche voice
                        of the factory whistle?!
And what could all the agents,
                          secret and double-secret,   375
do against the cobblestones
                         and flag of the proletariat!
When the people rose,
                   the empire was laid low.
You cannot change the people,
                          but the government can go.

Russian Ivans are terrible
                when they are indivisible,
when they understand
          that indeed
                 they are terrible!   380

5

Ivanovo, Ivanovo,
tears, tears that run over,
so full of sorrow, so,
so sick at heart and, oh,
tattered and torn Ivanovo,   385
battered and bruised Ivanovo,
drunk as a lord, Ivanovo,
victim of fraud, Ivanovo . . .
So went the jingle, or
maybe not, who knows . . .   390
but like a spark that falls
on cotton—what a blaze!

It was not the siren, loud-mouthed,
howled
            like a brawling serf;
in Ivanovo
            Ivan
                  howled   395
for all his Ivan's worth!
As the Tsar's resplendent eagle
has two separate noddles,
Ivan has only one,
and that one's
                  drink-befuddled.   400

But again
            the poor
are threatening

and in the furrows of their brow,
rebellion
        is brewing.

The serf
        is a worker   405
who at core is like a beast—
and the eyes in whose head
are blind beyond belief.
But he who, when he cudgels
his brains
                and breaks his back,   410
knows such a life is awful—
he's no slavish hack.

What is this Russian calico?
It's
    a love that sighs and sorrows
after the reds
                and blues   415
and pale pinks of the meadows.
The factories have dimmed
nature's face
                with their smoke,
yet pollen still clings
to smoke-draped thoughts.   420
All that the sly machine
took away from the peasants,
with a moist,
                floral
                        babble,
blooms in cotton prints.
Oh, calico from Ivanovo,   425
stirring in the breeze,
heavy with corn, full-voiced,
you are like the Russian fields.
Calico
        is the field's alms,

52

besprinkled with dew.   430
Calico
       is repentance
before Beauty duped.
Making eyes,
          people stroll,
dressed in cotton from Ivanovo,
calico for Easter-wear,   435
courting,
        leading to the altar.
Oh, calico from Ivanovo,
made of roses
        and rainbows,
you'll never wear right through—
the workers wear out
           before you.   440

Warp
     the yarn.
Bend
   the torso!
Spin,
    spin,
       spin
a web
   for yourself!
You hang so well   445
in the kingdom of calico—
how could the suicide
prefer
   hemp
      to cotton?
An old weaver slipped
on some little stone or other.   450
Is vodka like guilt,
what are you stumbling over?

Not expecting any doctor,
                        the weaver lies,
wipes his lips;
vodka's
          his whole life—   455
it's not just a drink.
They knocked up a coffin for the weaver,
they clubbed together for a sleigh.
The dead man was happy:
                        "At least
I am going to the graveyard in a gentlemanly way."   460
This summer the grass rose,
whispering above the mound,
but the dead weaver's penalties
were set down to his account.
It's a sin not to think,
                        but oh—   465
thinking is dreadful—
                        spare us, God!
Take away our woes,
River Uvod,
          River Uvod!
Howling sirens—
they know something's the matter—   470
spin,
      spin,
            spin
yourself a banner!

"My sweetheart is not meeting
some belle from the big city—
he's gone to a May Day meeting   475
on the banks of the Talka River.
To celebrate the workers' holiday
I'm accompanying my sweet,
I shall take off my red scarf

54

and bind it to a tree.   480
Until the time our baby boy
first sees the light of day,
oh little scarf,
              why don't you fly,
and make us banners brave!"
I must go to the meeting,
                    the May Day,
                              May Day
                                   meeting, 485
clutching, clutching a leaflet,
                    like a nestling, to my breast,
and catching the glint of metal,
                    from my calloused palm,
                              like a petal,
to blow away a lady-bird—
                    far from the flying lead.
I want to go to the Talka,
                    the river,
                         river
                              Talka,
even though by the enemy
                    beset, in bitter strife,   490
I'll get caught up in a skirmish,
                    where grim death keeps the
                                   tally,
with bullet and with whip,
                    with draw-bolt and with knife.
I must go to the strike,
              the strike,
                    the strike,
                              the strike,
the mighty stirring of
              the workers' arms and backs,
to egg them on with roars of
                    "Wheel away the damned
                              informers!"   495

Let him chew on the cotton,
                    the son of a bitch!
I want to see Frunze,
                    Frunze, but not in bronze—
him standing by a birch tree
                    that's been split by the storm,
even in May, red-faced,
                    as though the frost were biting,
wearing a Russian blouse
                    of stormy turquoise blue.   500

Meeting,
         meeting,
carry me,
         do!
The worker in Russia
is dynamite right through.
But when will it explode,   505
this dynamite?
And what will be its echo?
Whom will it annihilate?
To what date in the future
do you look ahead,   510
nineteen-o-five,
year of the dead?

Fyodor Afanasev,
nicknamed Father,
threw his cap on the ground,   515
as though his life were over,
as though among the pines,
on this May Day morning,
he saw
         the dancing bludgeons
of the Black Hundreds: 520
"I was born in a village,
Yazvishchi by name.

56

I wandered about this land,
I saw filth,
          I saw shame.
Only to someone blind in the eye   525
would it not be crystal-clear
where the main trouble lies,
that spawns all the others.
I shall die
          and you shall die,
and the fields will be full of the same rye,   530
but as for the Winter Palace,
                   will there
be the same ugly mugs there?"

And then along there came
one, Andrey Bubnov by name,
he'd a voice,
          this lad of nineteen,   535
like a flourish of factory sirens.
"In Russia we've got our sweet tooths,
but we've others who chew on iron,
and those others,
           what they like best,
is the wise guys' candy—
              power!   540
But the Tsars
          and all their fellows,
eaten away by rust,
have no power
          over the workers,
over the soul of Rus."

And maybe Pasha Postyshev,   545
though later he started to sweat,
was the first to shout out the slogan:
"All power to the Soviets!"

And Matryona Sarmenteva
cut in so vigorously   550
that the buttons flew from her blouse,
and
        the crows started up in the sky.
She flared: "Keep your big fiddling mitts
off my weaver's thighs, god damn it!
They call me a yokel, well nuts—   555
I'm a woman,
                you goats!
Those bunglers are knocking back vodka,
drunkenly selling out the people.
They're tormenting Russia like some yokel,
but she's a woman after all!"   560

Avenir Nozdrin was an etcher
and he also wrote poetry.
He straightened out the leaflet
and it began to speak.
The verse,
        awkward and uneven,   565
was not dressed in rhyme—it was free;
in any case, "People"
                and "Freedom"
are as near rhyme as need be!
"People,
        whom shall we elect
as chairman of our Soviet?   570
A drinker,
        but surely no liar,
why not let's have a poet!"
Years ago,
        the Russian people,
emphatically stressing the point,
said: "In Russia, the poet's
                a champion.   575

58

If he's not,
          then he's no poet."
Fame,
        what's fame worth?
It's a bitter,
            heavy mead.
He is famed
          who cast the word
among the people, silenced and weak!   580

Olya Genkina,
            Olya, Olechka!
They said: "Where are you going in the snow?
You'll get lost, Olya,
                like a needle
in the rotting haystack of Russia."
Smiling at those of little faith,   585
with her shining, clear blue eyes,
Olya Olechka
            conveyed
a case of guns
            to the weavers' town.
The porter had
            a bronze name plate,
the porter had
            an evil ratface,   590
which, with an air of simplicity,
he disguised,
          in childlike duplicity.
He too was a worker of sorts,
an Ivanovo man,
                not imported,
but his face was like
                a police-   595
sentry box
          standing over the country.
What he saw was a hat.

A ribbon.
White hands.
                A girl "antilectual".
You're too civil by far,
                        Olechka.
In his crude eyes
                this meant
                        "conspirator"   600
Your case weighs heavier than it ought to.
It gives me ideas, thought the porter.
He dropped the case in the crush
and yelled:
                "The damned bitch has got guns!"
And his colleagues
                rose up like ogres,   605
sniffing
        the sweet smell of a pogrom.
And hurled their hooks valiantly,
lacerating
        the girl's body.
They tear her to shreds,
                        like animals,
bellowing:
                "For Church and Fatherland!"   610
What is become of you, Olechka?
May you be cursed,
                just like enemy agents,
you phony workers
                who tear
the intelligentsia
                into fragments!
The Black Hundreds
                are phony workers,   615
false witnesses,
                a phony folk.
All, whose filthy destiny
                        it is

60

to guard the rotting gates.
And for the inveterate Black Hundreds,
inclined to butchery and more,   620
every thinking person in Russia
is a caseload of revolvers.

Such innocence in your flowers,
                              calico, calico!
As the nightingale's song,
                    is your breath.
But from what did this flowered print grow?   625
From the workers' blood,
                    from the workers' blood . . .
Calico, calico,
              miracle or horror?
That old weaver won't rise from beneath the sod,
but empires fall,
                  slithering
in the workers' blood,
                    in the workers' blood . . .   630

6

When the empress came to the field hospital,
to pluck at the lint and shed a tear,
midst all the white-winged Russian Lizas,
over the soldiers with their oozing pus,
Nicholas II sighed, for here   635
he at least could see, the empire was lost.
He clutched the "George" in the palm of his hand,
leaning over the bed, blood-streaked with vomit:
like a pale manikin in an icy land,
something still breathed and moaned upon it.   640
The eyes were two boreholes in the white,
the mouth was coated with the foam of convulsions.
"Tell me, my friend, is this the first time?"
"No, the second . . ."
                        "And when *was* the first?"

Clearly, the soldier didn't know his Tsar,   645
and croaked, without any sarcasm at all:
"Sunday,
        January
                the ninth
                        it were . . ."
The Tsar gave a shudder,
                and dropped the "George".

Among the people the Tsar was nicknamed "Bloody",
but there was something bloodless about him.   650
It seemed, even if you struck him,
with an air of indifference he'd hide his feelings.
His wife, indifferently he adored,
not begrudging her attachment to Rasputin.
With indifference,
                he lost one war   655
and half asleep now a second was losing.
And compared to him, even lank Fredericks,
with his yellowing grey hair, was ready,
inept as he was, now and then to take risks,
shedding scurf from his spangles into the coffee.   660
The Tsar tried,
                not being a cruel man at all,
to contain the blood-letting within decent limits,
but the source of the monarch's fall
was the lethal quality of his indifference.
Did it really have to take three centuries   665
to so reduce the power of authority
that strikes, with their strident voice, could bring
the rotten system to its knees?
Power lost its grip,
                there was such disorder
that even drugs from Tibet   670
Badmayev shoved down its throat did not restore
the flabby body of the state.

66

Everything degenerated,
                    there was chaos all around,
everything went to pieces,
                    thieves were everywhere.
But arrest the whole of Russia?
                    How?   675
Even the police
          were affected by inertia.
And the end of the empire came
when all the Khodynkas and Tsu-shimas
made up such a concentration of shame,
that this shame was too much to bear.   680
And the lonely royal train, hurtling
between Malaya Vishera and Dno,
encountered only insults, not deference,
like a blind dog trying to find its way home.
And clutching at the yellow silk upholstery,   685
the Tsar heard shots outside in the smoke,
                              and curses,
and a song unknown to him till then:
"Arise, ye downtrodden of the earth."
And people whispered advice into his ear:
"Why not ask England for a loan?"   690
But somewhere else the bayonets had dislodged
Repin's portrait from its white Duma home.
He recalled the letter to Meshchersky where
Tsar Peter
          —very cleverly for a mere youth—
described how he fell from a gondola,   695
comparing Venice to a prostitute.
"Russia's a fallen woman too,"
                    half asleep
the Tsar murmured, with a deathbed yawn.
All those who fall, in whatever country,
for that same reason call the country fallen.   700
The Tsar was tinlike,
                    like some inanimate thing.

In his absent gaze,
                    there was not a flicker.
When, like a gift
                    to Guchkov and Shulgin,
he typed out his abdication paper.
The monarchists, deeply offended   705
with the Tsar's lack of feeling, were disconsolate and glum:
"He gave up Russia, like some no-good officer,
a military disgrace, handing over his squadron."

A howling blizzard swept from the Urals,
a blizzard with compassion
                    and without it too.   710
The Tsar's tragedy went on to its dénouement.
The tragedy of Russia continued.
The Tsar was reluctant to venture outside—
he went only if the heir begged hard.
Through a crack, came a whisper,
                    and the fence cried: 715
"Look, the Tsar!
          Tsar Nicholas the Last!"
For the first time it dawned upon the Tsar
how the court upbringing had deluded him.
As a boy he'd been instructed by governesses
in tales by Perrault and the Brothers Grimm.   720
And now, without any foreign tongue, the heir,
turning Bolshevik news-sheets into toy boats
that had "S.O.S." writ all over them,
played with the sailor who was his dyadka.
He certainly put the old man through the mill: 725
"Dyadka, a story!"
                    "You really want one?
                              Wait . . .
Would you like the one about Ivan the Fool?"
"I would!"
          But by now it was too late.

7

When great Peter finally was brought
down by a terrible and fatal fever,   730
in his delirium, an axe he sought,
and spat blood, just like a worker.
His icy brow burned. On his back,
defenceless before death,
                    the Tsar,
not like a headsman, groped for an axe,   735
but rather like an obsessive carpenter.
Rending space with his mighty arm,
deliriously he muttered through the pain,
"My lord, so much is yet undone!
So much is still unshaped."   740
Again the Tsar, from the opening void,
threw himself back into the feast,
and shaking with savage laughter, fed
his guests cat,
            fox,
                    and wolf meat.
In the end he took to his bed,   745
as though the wolf had choked him,
and there appeared the Russian god,
like a chained prisoner, before him.
And asking for paradise,
meek
        and resigned,
                    the monarch   750
signed his last ukase:
Freedom for those in prison camps.
God took the ukase,
                    but he shook
his head,
        he had no faith in Tsars;
and death, grinning crookedly,   755
granted the Tsar one minute more.

And so, two words
                alone remain
of this last will and testament:
"Give everything . . . ,"
                   but give to whom,
the Tsar had no time . . .
                    his hand fell.   760
What would he have gone on to pen?
"To the people . . ."?
                The mystery is insoluble.
But where
         is there a definition
of the people, cast in metal?
The people cannot be contained   765
in an ukase—there is no definition.
Like genius,
            the people cannot be explained.
It transcends the bounds of explanation.
But beyond the line of kings
              and queens,
and all that gorged
            and fell away,   770
from the most absolute Russian features,
the face of the fatherland took shape.
"Give everything . . ."—
             the peasant and
the factory hand made the same deduction,
accustomed to all that life cast up,   775
only to freedom unaccustomed.
And shaking the very earth's axis,
approaching nineteen-seventeen,
came the resounding cry,
              "Give everything . . ."
and a distant echo,
           ". . . to the people."   780

72

8

And so we grew
without a sou,
a bitter taste
            upon our tongues,
tattered Ivans
who had to stand   785
more than
            a mortal may endure.
Ivan the Fool
is canny—
            you'll
never buy him with lying tales.
Hard times are here,   790
pregnant, they bear
the start of all the future ages.
Hacked to pieces,
wracked and steeped in
our own salty blood, we lift   795
our heads up, lofted
on the gibbet,
as we whisper:
            "Russia, live!"
And she survived,
she will survive,   800
like a bright cornflower in the rye.
Nothing's sublimer,
nothing higher
than truth that has survived the lie.
All the brute force   805
of Tsar and lord
passed,
            without crushing you at all,
limitless,
rebellious,
gentle, tender Russian soul.   810

75

Be it renowned
that lovely land,
where truth shall never pass away.
Long may that great,
good potentate,
the people, live
                —and long hold sway!

815

EPILOGUE

In the history of Russia there are pages
filled with beauty and with suffering;
and as in cotton prints, you cannot tell
where blood ends and flowers begin.   820
He who is no historian
                          is no poet.
We are all Pimens,
                     though at some remove,
and to reconstruct the decades that have flown
is no less task
                   than making history.
But to come after
                     always is a curse,   825
leading to obtuseness, crude lack of subtlety.
I shall never count as Russians those
who do not know Russian history.
Nor shall I count as Russians those
who shun ideas for pride's false salvation,   830
who possess neither the peasant's robust constitution,
nor your tremendous strength,
                                oh working class.
Remain unsullied,
                   proletarian firmament!
On the sites of Bratsk,
                     BAM,
                          and KamAZ,
I saw the workers' power ferment—   835

I believe in the conscience of the working class.
He is no Russian who so loves his comfort,
his car,
          his fridge,
                     his fancy clothes,
                                 his rings,
that he has forgotten, as he buys up icons,
what songs the Russian revolution sings.   840
He is no Russian
                  who to the heroic ranks
elevates only Russians,
                        puffing out his chest,
he for whom Saint Joan is nothing special,
nor John Brown,
                Fuchik
                       or Anne Frank.
Russia's strength lies in this:
                                 her victories   845
as she advances, have not made her vain.
All humankind's experience she takes in,
while still remaining Russia all the same.
History is given to us so we
need not repeat it, to our own great risk.   850
And irresistible is the lovely law of History:
"He who was nothing will be everything."

Arise, my son!
                Arise, my little Peter!
Your alarm clock is ringing.
                              Put your satchel on!
Don't be a stranger in your own country.   855
(Yesenin lied to himself when he spoke so.)
It is a sin and it is cause for shame
to be ignorant
               of your identity,
                                  your origin.
In history such cowardly blanks

produce a blankness in our children.   860
I tell myself:
            "Don't become a spiritual vacuum.
Be more open with this child of yours."
Fathers,
            don't fear the coming generations.
You will lose your children,
                              if you fear them.
Arise, my son!
            Burst through the ages.   865
Be equal to our Russian history.
Ivan Fyodorov's letters on the pages
of your textbooks—
            do not let them lie.
Let neither vainglory nor love of comfort chain us.
Advancing to meet the coming centuries,   870
give everything in Russia
                        to the children,
and they will give to Russia everything.

NOTES

l. 40 *Susanin*: Ivan Susanin (d. 1613), legendary hero of the war of liberation against the Polish intervention during the Time of Troubles (1604-13); sacrificing himself for the newly elected Tsar Michael, he led the Polish army into impassable marshes. He appears also in oral folklore, as well as in Glinka's opera *A Life for the Tsar* (renamed *Ivan Susanin* after the Revolution). A popular symbol of patriotism, Susanin is here linked with Ivan the Fool's tale, which is similarly leading the enemy, the ruling class in this case, into a deadly impasse.

l. 44 *kvass*: A sour drink made of rye bread or flour with malt (bread kvass), or a fizzing drink of berries, fruit or honey.

l. 51 *Koshchey*: An evil and miserly being in Russian folklore, generally represented as a tall, thin old man; the epithet usually applied to him is "deathless" or "immortal" (*bessmertny*). As the miserly preserver of certain treasures, he plays a role similar to that of the serpent or dragon referred to earlier in the poem. Both are enemies of the folklore heroes and are virtually interchangeable, the struggle with them being, among other things, a symbolic representation of the Christianization of Russia.

l. 52 *shchi*: Cabbage soup.

l. 61 *Lord Ivan Vasilevich*: Ivan IV, the Terrible (1530-84), first Grand Duke of Muscovy to assume the title of Tsar of Russia. (For his autocratic ambitions and increasing paranoia, see notes on ll. 88, 97, 185 below.)

ll. 82-8 *"Aye, it is true . . . faith in that!"*: In this passage, the nightingale's *strast* (passion, love, song, poetry, etc.) is contrasted with the Tsar's *vlast* (power, authority, etc.), a juxtaposition which was to be traditional in Russia (e.g. Pushkin and his "patron", Tsar Nicholas). Poetry, then, is subversive, "heresy", and always a threat to authority in its various manifestations. Here, the Tsar's exalted view that he held his throne from God is at issue: Ivan obsessively sought confirmation in the Scriptures and Old Slavonic Chronicles for the doctrine of the divine right of kings.

l. 94 *Viskovaty*: Ivan Viskovaty, a member of the Chosen Council which effectively governed Russia in Ivan IV's name up to 1560, functioned as the Tsar's personal secretary, secretary for foreign affairs, and chief diplomat. He was nevertheless executed in a horrible manner in 1570, having bravely petitioned the increasingly psychopathic monarch to put an end to the bloodshed.

l. 97 *oprichniks*: The Tsar's bodyguards, somewhat like Turkish janissaries; from the old Russian word for "special" or "apart". From 1565 till his death, the increasingly distrustful Ivan entrenched himself within that part of the state, comprising certain towns and districts, and even sections of Moscow, specially designated for the maintenance of his court and household, which was initially composed of some 1000 carefully selected nobles, known as *oprichniki*, with their families.

l. 110 *Ivan Fyodorov*: (d. 1583) Known as *pervopechatnik* (the first printer). In 1563 (over 100 years after Gutenberg), a special printing office was opened in Moscow, in the Church of St Nicholas in the Kremlin, where Ivan Fyodorov had been deacon, and in 1564 Ivan Fyodorov and Pyotr Mstislavtsev produced the first printed book, *Apostol* (The Apostle). They were harassed by the copyists or ecclesiastical authorities who accused them of heresy, and fled to Lithuania.

l. 185 *Kurbsky*: Prince Andrey Kurbsky (1528-83), politician, soldier and humanist writer and translator; leader of the boyar opposition to Ivan. In the 1540s and '50s, he was one of Ivan IV's closest friends, a member of the Chosen Council, an exalted functionary and general. However, fearing imminent arrest after the fall of Adashev's government in 1564, he fled to Lithuania, where the Polish king granted him lands. The same year, he actually led a Polish army against Russia.

l. 198 *brooms . . . dog-masks*: A reference to the oprichniks, who wore dog masks and carried brooms, attached to the saddle, as a symbol of their role as destroyers and sweepers-away of traitors.

l. 201 *torn nostrils*: The men who waylay the printer are established as outlaws or highwaymen, whose leader has had his nostrils torn, a common form of torture for captured bandits.

l. 249 *Lefort*: Frants Lefort (1656-99), Russian statesman of Swiss origin. In 1675, he came to Russia as a soldier and took part in the campaigns against the Crimean Tatars and Turks in the '80s. From about 1690, he was a boon companion of the Tsar's, but though very influential, played no part in governmental matters. Though the Lefortovo Prison in Moscow is named after him, Lefort never actually took part in the brutalities Peter the Great forced upon so many of his nobles. He remained always a Western man.

l. 250 *Peter*: Peter I (the Great) (1682-1725) in effect deserved the epithet "Terrible" more than his predecessor, Ivan IV (see note on l.291 below: his revenge against the Streltsy).

l. 259 *Menshikov*: Aleksandr Menshikov (?1673-1729), favourite of Peter the Great and Catherine. In his youth he is reputed to have sold pies (*pirogi*) in the streets of Moscow (see ll. 263-4). Lefort, who had taken Menshikov into his service, introduced him to Peter, and from 1697 the two were inseparable. Eventually Menshikov's influence began to exceed Lefort's. He rose to the rank of Field-Marshal in the army and become a Russian Prince. Later, he concentrated on internal questions, collaborating with Peter on the extensive reforms. Menshikov was, however, a notorious bribe-taker and embezzler of public funds, and the old aristocracy finally managed to turn Peter's successor, Catherine, against him. He died in exile.

l. 274 *Rus*: Name of the Eastern Slavonic tribes. From the ninth century and the beginning of the early feudal state, the name Rus became also the name for the state and the nation.

l. 287 *Anna*: Anna Mons (d. 1714), daughter of a German goldsmith or wine merchant from the German quarter of Moscow. Lefort found her for Peter, whose mistress she became. The Tsar, finding her a relief from his pious wife Eudoxia, divorced the latter and even thought of marrying Anna.

l. 291 *Streltsy*: Members of an infantry corps (musketeers), instituted by Ivan IV around 1550, under special jurisdiction and enjoying special privileges, they functioned as a regular army and military arm of the Tsar. Peter, however, feared their power and wanted to build an army more immediately beholden to himself. The Streltsy were opposed to the Tsar's westernizing reforms and their opposition increased when he dispersed them as the Moscow garrison, sending them away from their families and estates to frontier towns. In 1698, while Peter was abroad, many Streltsy deserted, returning to Moscow, and an abortive siege of the capital followed. Though many of the rebels were hanged or banished, Peter was not satisfied and, on his own return in 1700, had the exiles brought back to Moscow. They were roasted over slow fires till they "confessed" (hence, perhaps, the reference at l. 285 to *felos de se*). Peter personally decapitated the first five mutineers, also insisting that his associates, like Menshikov, join him in the beheadings.

l. 329 *oprichnina*: A collective term for the *oprichniki* and also for the territory assigned to them (see note on l. 97).

l. 334 *Muromets*: Ilya Muromets, the chief character among the heroes (*bogatyrs*) of the Kiev cycle of epic folk songs (*byliny*), *circa* tenth century A.D. He is portrayed as defender of the common people, religion and land.

l. 335 *Buslayev*: Vasily Buslayev, a boisterous giant or *bogatyr*, who figures in the *byliny* connected with the trading city of Novgorod. Buslayev seems to reflect the popular opposition to merchant domination of the city.

l. 340 *Razin*: Stepan (Stenka is a diminutive) Razin (*c.*1630-71), a Don Cossack who led a mixed Russian and non-Russian peasant, colonial-type rebellion (1670-1) of the needy and more newly arrived escapees from serfdom, the rebellion engulfing the south-eastern steppe region. This formidable uprising was one of the periodic frontier rebellions against the serf-based regime of the centralizing state (see also notes on ll. 340, 341 below). The aim of the leaders was to reach Moscow, destroy the power of the privileged town authorities and the boyars and, extending Cossack democracy, to establish some kind of direct link between the people and the sovereign. With considerable difficulty, Moscow finally suppressed the revolt, after which Don Cossack independence was largely reduced. The vision of this and other popular uprisings, however much they might lack any clear political orientation, was nevertheless a terrifying one for the governing classes.

l. 340 *Bolotnikov*: Ivan Bolotnikov (d. 1608), serf-born leader during the Time of Troubles of the first (1606-7) of the four great peasant revolts against the central State in the south-east and middle Volga frontier regions. Bolotnikov's movement to a certain extent, and unlike the others, succeeded in provoking a mass rising in the centre. Also unlike the others, in its early stages it was not headed by Don or Ural Cossacks, but was a revolutionary rising of the lowest classes rather than primarily of the peasants.

l. 341 *Pugachov*: Emelyan Pugachov (*c.*1742-75), a Don Cossack, leader of the fourth great peasant rebellion, in the reign of Catherine II, against the central power and the serf-owners. It started not as a rebellion of serfs but of Cossacks protesting against their diminished autonomy. Non-Russians joined Pugachov on a massive scale; as did the new eighteenth-century class of serfs working as mine and metal workers in the Urals. Pugachov voiced the aspirations and resentments of the underdogs, the common people, against the rapacious gentry, who were portrayed as a kind of archetypal, un-Christian foe. Like Razin, Pugachov went down in folklore as the defender of the poor, a benevolent, divinely protected magician-warrior.

l. 342 *the marks of a king*: Pugachov masqueraded as the Emperor Peter, Catherine the Great's husband, who was deposed and then murdered in 1762. He evidently bore some "royal marks" on his body, which he showed to the crowd to prove the legitimacy of his claim. As has been suggested (see note on l. 340), the rebels were not against the Tsar, only his nobles. From the first False Dmitry, the supposed son of Ivan the Terrible, there was a long line of pretender Tsars seeking to legitimize their rebellions in this way.

l. 344 *rushlights*: These typified the humble peasant hut from which a great national genius like the first printer had come.

88

l. 350 *Pushkin*: It is to be noted that Pushkin gave (in the circumstances of official censorship) a surprisingly sympathetic portrait of Pugachov in his story, "The Captain's Daughter" (1836). He also wrote a history of the rebellion.

l. 352 *birch-bark proclamations*: The first, or very early, Russian documents, discovered near Novgorod, were written on birch bark.

l. 365 *Tsar's drinking-house*: All drinking establishments were under the control of the crown, forming an important source of revenue. There is a sudden shift of scene here to the revolutionary period.

l. 366 *Lena*: In 1912, a strike for better working conditions was organized among the workers in the Lena goldfields in Siberia. Shortly after, 12,000 workers marched to the administration buildings to protest the arrest of their leaders. Tsarist troops opened fire and hundreds were killed or wounded.

l. 366 *Winter Palace*: A mass demonstration on Sunday, 9 January 1905, was led by the Orthodox priest, Father Georgy Gapon (1870-1906), to the Tsar's palace in St Petersburg, where it was intended to present the monarch with a petition—again, as with Razin and others, an attempt to establish a direct line of communication between throne and populace—demanding a Constituent Assembly and complete civil and political freedom. Though in fact the crowd was unarmed, the government lost its head and troops fired, inflicting serious casualties. The massacre, known thereafter as "Bloody Sunday", finally destroyed the age-old belief in the Emperor's essential love and concern for his people.

ll. 370-3 *Putilov works . . . Gapons*: The strike at the Putilov works in St Petersburg in January 1905 resulted from the dismissal of four men who belonged to the Petersburg Society of Russian Factory and Workshop Workers, which had existed since 1903 with the official encouragement of the Petersburg police, and whose president was now Father Gapon. As with the earlier experiments in "police socialism", the Zubatov unions, founded by Sergey Zubatov (1864-1917), a former revolutionary, who became head of the Moscow branch of the Tsarist security police, the intention was to divert social unrest into officially controllable channels. In fact, the unions became penetrated by Social Democratic forces, Father Gapon himself playing a double role as police agent and revolutionary organizer. While at first the strikers' demands were economic, the mood quickly became revolutionary and led to the demonstration before the Winter Palace (see note on l. 366).

l. 371 *Morozov*: Savva Morozov (d. 1905) was an industrialist and Bolshevik benefactor.

l. 374 *veche*: An assembly of the citizens of the large towns, first heard of during the Kievan period, late eleventh century. In the twelfth century, it became politically and even diplomatically more influential, especially in Novgorod. where it was an assembly of all the citizens and, in theory, held supreme power.

l. 381 *Ivanovo*: The main town in the Ivanovo province (*oblast*) of the RSFSR, north-east of Moscow on the Volga, Ivanovo (Ivanovo-Voznesensk up to 1932), the "Russian Manchester", figures in Yevtushenko's original title for this poem, *Ivanovskiye sitsy* (Calico from Ivanovo). The largest textile centre after Moscow, it was also an important centre of the labour movement from the 1880s and a significant Bolshevik stronghold. In 1905, the celebrated Ivanovo-Voznesensk strike, at first economic but swiftly politicized, occurred, during which one of the first Soviets of Workers' Deputies was elected. This body implemented freedom of assembly, speech and the press, and established a revolutionary order in the town, taking steps to help the strikers and their families; an armed workers' detachment was also formed. Among the organizers of the strike and the Soviet were M. V. Frunze and others mentioned in the poem. Later, in 1914-18, a revolutionary movement again sprang up in Ivanovo-Voznesensk. In March 1917, another Soviet of Workers' Deputies was elected, and later a detachment of Worker Red Guards from Ivanovo and nearby Shuya took part in the October uprising in Moscow.

l. 468 *River Uvod*: Ivanovo is situated on this river. There is a pun here on the Russian word *uvodit*, meaning "to take or lead away".

l. 476 *Talka River*: Workers' meetings were held here, when troops sent by the provincial governor prevented strikers meeting openly in Ivanovo-Voznesensk. On 3 June 1905, participants in one such meeting were fired upon by troops, the general strike (see note on l. 381) continuing, however. The whole of this passage is in *chastushka* (i.e. popular folk-song) style and is spoken by the worker's girl-friend.

l. 495 *informers*: This refers to the custom of putting police spies and other renegades on a wheelbarrow and wheeling them out of the factory.

l. 497 *Frunze*: Mikhail Frunze (1885-1925) played an important part in the workers' movement in Ivanovo-Voznesensk in 1905 and again in 1917. He joined the Bolshevik organization in 1904 and in 1905 was sent by the Moscow Bolshevik Committee to the Ivanovo-Voznesensk region, where he worked with textile workers in Shuya. The Shuya-Ivanovo armed workers' detachment, created by him, took part in the armed uprising in Moscow in December 1905. In September 1917, Frunze became chairman of the Soviet of Workers', Soldiers' and Peasants' Deputies in Shuya and led the detachment of Red Guards (see note on l. 381) which fought in the October 1917 battles in Moscow. Rising to be Chief-of-Staff of the Red Army, Frunze died shortly after an operation for a stomach ulcer which, it was widely rumoured in Moscow, Stalin had persuaded him to undergo unnecessarily so that he could appoint his friend Voroshilov in his place. There was so much confusing talk that the Party organization in Ivanovo-Voznesensk demanded an inquiry.

Frunze here evidently represents the revolutionary purity of the early days, before the hypocritical erection of bronze memorials honouring the dead heroes of the Revolution.

l. 513 *Fyodor Afanasev*: (1859-1905). One of his pseudonyms was "Father". Born into a peasant family, Afanasev organized Social Democratic revolutionary circles among Petersburg and Moscow textile workers. By 1896, he was active in the unification of Social Democratic organizations in Ivanovo-Voznesensk, Shuya and other towns, and was arrested in 1903. In 1904, he was living illegally in Ivanovo and became secretary of the Ivanovo-Voznesensk Committee of the Party. With Frunze he was one of the leaders of the 1905 Ivanovo-Voznesensk strike and was killed during a meeting on the Talka River by a band of Black Hundreds (see note on l. 520 below) and Cossacks.

l. 520 *Black Hundreds*: So called by their opponents, these bands of extreme right-wing opponents of the revolutionary workers' movement were notorious for their anti-Semitism (and anti-intellectualism). Recruited from minor tradesmen or non-factory working class elements (e.g. the porters mentioned later in the poem), these *pogromshchiki* were little more than mobs, incited by "patriotic" monarchist and police organizations.

l. 534 *Andrey Bubnov*: (1883-1940). Born in Ivanovo-Voznesensk, his father the manager of a textile factory, he became a Party member in 1903 and in 1905 was elected to the Ivanovo-Voznesensk Party Committee. Arrested many times before the Revolution, Bubnov played a leading role after it, as commissar on several fronts during the Civil War. With Trotsky's defeat, he became head of the Political Administration of the Red Army. In 1929 he replaced Lunacharsky as Commissar of Education, which he remained until his arrest and execution in the 1937 purge, along with most of the other old revolutionaries.

l. 545 *Postyshev*: Pavel (Pasha) Postyshev (1887-1939), born into a textile worker's family, was a member of the Party from 1904. In 1905, Postyshev was elected a deputy of the Ivanovo-Voznesensk Soviet. In 1908, he was arrested and sentenced to hard labour, and in 1912 was permanently exiled to Irkut. Active in the Civil War, Postyshev rose to be Secretary of the Ukrainian Party organization, assisting Stalin in the 1934 purges in the Ukraine and again in 1937-9. However, according to Khrushchev in his famous de-Stalinizing speech at the Twentieth Party Congress in 1956, Postyshev had serious misgivings about the arrests and, expressing these forcefully, was demoted to a provincial position in 1938, Khrushchev, in fact, replacing him on the Secretariat and Orgburo. He was arrested and either tried in secret and shot, or shot without trial. Again according to Khrushchev, he was among the few brave men to refuse to make a false confession.

l. 549 *Matryona Sarmenteva*: A deputy to the Ivanovo-Voznesensk Soviet in 1905.

l. 561 *Avenir Nozdrin*: (1862-1938). Born in Ivanovo-Voznesensk, the son of a salesman, he worked as an engraver in a textile factory. He was elected chairman of the Ivanovo-Voznesensk Soviet in 1905. Nozdrin started publishing poetry in the Nineties. Much of his work was dedicated to the revolutionary cause and the workers' lot, especially in the Ivanovo-Voznesensk struggle. Under such titles as "On the Eve of May", "Our Talka", "At the Meeting", "The Ring of Chains", they described the experience of a revolutionary pursued by the Tsarist government. His *Selected Poems* appeared in 1937. A victim of the purges in 1938, Nozdrin has been posthumously rehabilitated.

l. 581 *Genkina*: Olga (Olya) Genkina's surname shows she was Jewish, hence the attack on her of the porters, "Black Hundreds" elements (see note on l. 520).

l. 593 *a worker of sorts*: See note on l. 520.

l. 598 *"antilectual"*: A neologism in Russian, unintentional probably, betraying the porter's ignorance, though possibly also expressing his sneering contempt for *intellectuals*.

l. 607 *hooks*: Special hooks used by porters in Russia to hitch things over their shoulders.

l. 637 *the "George"*: A military order, one of the commonest, often given to those who had been wounded. The scene, of course, has shifted to World War I and the last moments of empire.

l. 647 *"Sunday, January the ninth"*: Bloody Sunday, 1905 (see note on l. 366).

l. 649 *"Bloody"*: The Tsar earned the nickname, "Bloody Nicholas", as a result of the forceful suppression of the 1905 insurrections.

l. 655 *one war*: That is, the Russo-Japanese War of 1904-5, over the question of Russian influence in Southern Manchuria and Japanese in Korea. Though Russia was unprepared for a war, the Tsar permitted himself to be swayed and handed over power to Admiral Alekseyev with headquarters in Port Arthur, demanding a free hand in Manchuria while denying Japan the same in Korea. After the breaking off of diplomatic relations in February 1904, Japan made a surprise attack on Russian warships at Port Arthur. Thereafter, the war was a series of Russian disasters, first by sea and then by land. In January 1905, Port Arthur was forced to capitulate. The war was finally brought to an end, Japan being under economic strain and Russia unwilling to divert additional forces to the Far East in view of growing revolutionary unrest in the centre.

l. 657 *Fredericks*: Count V. B. Fredericks (1838-1922), Minister of the Imperial Court from 1897 to 1917. Of Swedish descent, Fredericks nevertheless was regarded by the public as a member of the Empress's unpopular German circle. He was the only witness to Nicholas's signing of the Draft Manifesto (see note on l. 682), in effect establishing a constitutional monarchy, just prior to the abdication in March 1917.

l. 671 *Badmayev*: P. A. Badmayev (1851-1919), a Buryat-Mongolian adventurer and well-known quack doctor in fashionable Petersburg circles, who had access to the Tsar. In 1893, he was of assistance to the future Prime Minister, Count Witte, in persuading the Tsar of the urgent need for a Trans-Siberian Railway, Badmayev, in fact, wanting the line extended through Mongolia, to facilitate stirring up a revolt of Tibetan, Chinese and Mongolian subjects of the Manchu dynasty.

l. 678 *all the Khodynkas and Tsu-shimas*: Khodynka was the field near Moscow, where in May 1896 over 1200 people were crushed to death in a mass stampede during the celebration of Nicholas II's coronation, thus marking his reign with disaster at the very outset. The Tsar's evident impassivity after this event was taken as a sign of his indifference to the fate of his subjects.

Tsu-shima was the island off which the Japanese fleet in May 1905 engaged the Russian Baltic fleet, sent by the Tsar to China in an attempt to regain mastery of the seas during the Russo-Japanese War (see note on l. 655), and inflicted a decisive defeat on it.

l. 682 *Malaya Vishera and Dno*: Malaya Vishera is a stop south-east of Petrograd on the Petrograd-Moscow line; Dno is a junction south of Petrograd, between Bologoye and Pskov. As Supreme Commander, Nicholas II, whose GHQ (*Stavka*) was located in Mogilev, conducted the war from his royal train and went back and forth between Petrograd and the front.

This passage refers to the complicated events in the days preceding the abdication on 2 March 1917, after the February revolution. Since the Emperor, who was at GHQ in Mogilev, did not respond to pressures for the appointment of a popular Prime Minister, the moderate-constitutionalist President of the Fourth Duma, Rodzyanko, approached the military commanders to support political demands. The Emperor ordered reliable troops to be sent to Petrograd to suppress the uprising. At the same time, he wanted to return to his family in Tsarskoye Selo. His train was routed through Malaya Vishera, to avoid the more direct Petrograd line from Mogilev which, it was expected, would carry the troops to the capital to put down the rising. On the journey news was received that a

93

Provisional Government had been formed in Petrograd and the Emperor's train, which had continued north as far as Malaya Vishera, returned to Bologoye junction and proceeded west, through Dno, to Pskov, headquarters of the Northern Front. There, however, the Emperor found the commander, General Ruzsky, as intent as Alekseyev, Commander-in-Chief, on persuading him to make political concessions. Alekseyev, in fact, sent the Emperor a draft manifesto, establishing a constitutional monarchy, a course repugnant to the Tsar, whose will, however, was broken and who agreed to sign it. This concession was too late and demands for his abdication followed immediately.

l. 692 *Repin's portrait*: This evidently refers to the removal of the Tsar's portrait by I. Y. Repin (1844-1930) from the Tauride Palace in Petrograd where the Duma met.

l. 701-2 *tinlike . . . not a flicker*: The Emperor's alleged impassivity (see also note on l. 678) was remarked upon by those present during the abdication crisis. Guchkov (see note on l. 703 below) referred to the "matter-of-factness" of the whole momentous affair, the Tsar's apparent failure to appreciate the scale of the tragedy that was engulfing his dynasty.

ll. 703-8 *Guchkov and Shulgin . . . squadron"*: A. I. Guchkov (1862-1936) and V. V. Shulgin (b. 1878) were the two Duma deputies who volunteered to travel to Pskov to try to settle the question of the formation of a new government and also, perhaps, negotiate the abdication (see note on l. 682). After General Ruzsky had obtained Nicholas's agreement to the abdication, the Emperor's staff, appalled at the hastiness of it all, managed to get the telegrams to Rodzyanko and to Alekseyev held up until the arrival of Guchkov and Shulgin, in the unrealized hope that the latter would be more accommodating. Guchkov, however, insisting that it was futile to send forces from the front to crush the revolutionary movement, the Emperor astonished everyone by announcing that he would abdicate for himself *and* for his son, since he did not want to be separated from the latter. His readiness to abdicate came as a great surprise to the Duma representatives and a great shock to the court, one of his generals remarking: "How is it possible to relinquish a throne just as if one were handing over the command of a cavalry squadron to another officer?"

l. 709 *Urals*: The scene has shifted to Yekaterinburg (now Sverdlovsk) in the Urals, where the Tsar and his family were summarily executed. They had been removed to Tobolsk in Siberia by Kerensky, Prime Minister of the Provisional Government, but soon after the Bolshevik October revolution, they were transferred to Yekaterinburg. The execution was probably precipitated by the advance of anti-Bolshevik forces threatening to take the place. The "heir" referred to below is of course Nicholas's son, the haemophiliac Tsarevich, Alexis.

l. 724 *dyadka*: Literally "uncle"; here it refers to the male equivalent of a governess, often a retired soldier or sailor who was responsible for the military side of a noble youth's education.

ll. 741-4 *Again the Tsar . . . wolf meat*: Peter the Great was in the habit of feigning sickness or near death as a means of finding out what his ministers and courtiers really thought about him. This describes one such grotesque incident.

l. 759 *"Give everything"*: On his deathbed, Peter pardoned all convicts not guilty of capital offences and all those, except murderers, sentenced to death for military offences. He wrote the words "Give everything" and then could write no more, sending for his daughter Anne to take down his last will and testament. When she arrived, he had fallen into a coma, but it is generally agreed that what he had in mind was a clear directive regarding the succession to the throne.

l. 822 *Pimen*: Father Pimen appears in Scene 5 of Pushkin's verse play, *Boris Godunov*. His opening speech is among the most famous lines in the play. A saintly chronicler, Pimen is about to embark on the final episode in his writings and to bear witness to Godunov's guilt as murderer of Ivan IV's son, Dimitri. The anchorite is portrayed as the selfless and truthful accuser of Godunov when all the world trembles before the latter.

l. 834 *Bratsk, BAM, and KamAZ*: Yevtushenko has written poems about all three. Bratsk is a hydro-electric power station constructed on the Angava, in Siberia; completed in 1964, it was the largest in the world. BAM is the Baikal-Amur Highway, a great project which has been under construction for several years. KamAZ is an automobile plant on the river Kama.

l. 839 *icons*: Icon-collecting typifies the Soviet *nouveaux riches*. It is a good way of investing money.

l. 844 *Fuchik*: Julius Fuchik (1903-43), Czech writer, politician, journalist, joined the original Czech Communist Party organization in 1921. A member of the underground Central Committee of the Czech Party, he was arrested by the Nazis and deported to Germany, where he was executed. While in prison, he wrote his famous book, *Report with the Rope round my Neck*. He has become a legendary Communist hero.

l. 856 *Yesenin*: A reference to a poem by Sergey Yesenin (1895-1925), *Vozvrashcheniye na Rodinu* (Return to my Home), which expresses a sense of alienation from the poet's peasant origins. But in another poem, *Letter to Yesenin*, Yevtushenko defends Yesenin as someone far truer to the Revolution than the Party hacks of the time who persecuted him.

DATE DUE